BIGGER PICTURE

Hands-on, how-to guide for creative children

Bigger Picture Book
By Eleanor Knauer

Published by Home School Art Book Group
www.HomeSchoolArtBookGroup.com

Design by STUDIO H Advertising & Design

Cover Art by Light Waves Video - Background Courtesy NASA/JPL-Caltech
ALBERT EINSTEIN and related rights ™/© of Hebrew University of Jerusalem, used under license. Represented exclusively by GreenLight.

ISBN: 097087100-7
Printed in the USA
www.BiggerPictureBook.com

Table of contents

Introduction

Creativity is manifested and comes to life in children's art. It serves as an invaluable tool of inspiration that helps young people understand how art, science, math and nature are all connected to "The Bigger Picture."

Using this book will help you teach children how to explore their creativity and expand their imagination. As you move through each chapter, let your students experience the process of creating by using various mediums and techniques to produce their own artistic expressions. This book will allow you to focus on techniques and provides examples to guide you through the creative process.

Art is found in every aspect of life and illustrated most beautifully through the eyes of a child. Enjoy watching the wonder in a child's face as the "Bigger Picture" comes to life.

"There are no seven wonders of the world in the eyes of a child. There are seven million."

WALT STREIGHTIFF

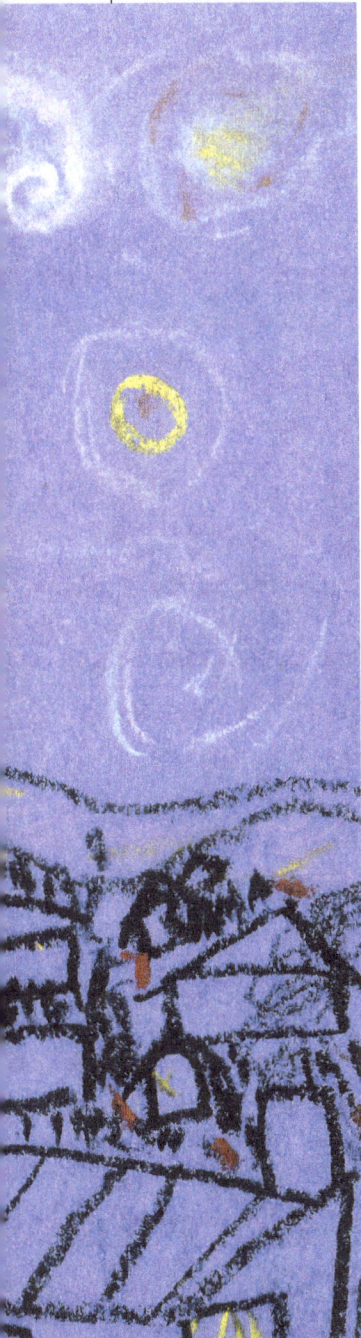

Cesar

The Importance of Elementary Art

A stimulating engagement with art during the elementary years has a significant impact on creative thinking for a lifetime. Creativity and art allow the brain to make connections in unique ways.

KEYS TO CREATIVITY

Make connections between ideas

Take advantage of change or chance

Recognize patterns

Construct networks

Take risks for your ideas

See things in new ways

CREATIVITY BUSTERS

Hovering

Evaluation/Comparison

Rewards/Excessive use of prizes

Competition

Restricting Choice

CREATIVITY BOOSTERS

Play games - change the rules to develop strategy

Encourage writing

Answer and ask questions

Encourage them to make/see connections

See things from different points of view

Be a good observer

Notice important details

Set deadlines to avoid over thinking

4th Grade

Kindergarten

5th Grade

The Creative Process for Kids

"Art is a personal expression
that is conveyed in many forms,
including but not limited to painting,
drawing, photography, sculpture,
printmaking, music, dancing, film
and literature. Although subjective,
art is appreciated for its ability to
stimulate the brain and speak
to the human spirit."

Kathleen Cavender, artist

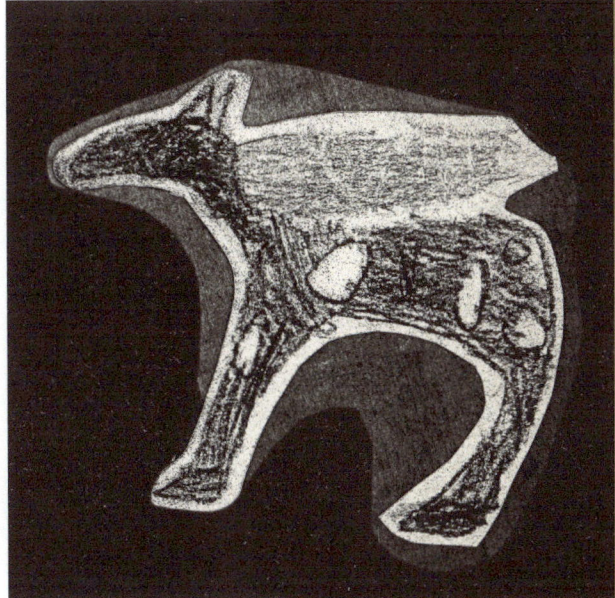

What if?

Innovation, Imagination, Creativity

Playing "What if" uses our growing knowledge of the bigger picture to create something completely new.

Look at this picture and ask yourself, "What if I:"

Moved the center?

Made it bigger? Or smaller?

Changed the colors?

Saw it at a different angle?

Made it symmetrical?

Angled the horizon?

Cropped the scene?

Repeated some other patterns?

Art Rules

Try these three simple rules for easy, fast, and pleasing results.

1. Make it as big as you can.
2. Fill the entire picture.
3. Make something happen in your picture.

Rule #1

Make It As Big As You Can **Over the Edge**

The process of artistic discovery is realized by making images that are taken right over the edges of the paper. While making images "as big as we can", and exceeding the boundaries, we overcome the sense that everything should be contained within the frame.

To get an expansive feeling of going beyond and out of the picture, have your students place the paper that is to be drawn upon on top of a larger sheet of paper or newspaper and have them make an image as large as possible. When the picture is finished and lifted off of the larger bottom sheet, the picture has gone "Over the Edge."

Cowboy looking at coyote tracks – 3rd Grade

Rule #1

Make It As Big As You Can **Art and Language**

Art is a unique language that can be read. Archeologists believe that prehistoric human drawings predate the written language, or mark making, by about ten thousand years.

As early as first grade, we can begin to use the term "subject" and children are able to identify it. Like the subject in a sentence, the subject of our picture will typically be a noun.

Rule #1

Make It As Big As You Can
Closure

The process of artistic discovery is realized by making images that are taken right over the edges of the paper. While making images "as big as we can", and exceeding the boundaries, we overcome the sense that everything should be contained within the frame.

To get an expansive feeling of going beyond and out of the picture, have your students place the paper that is to be drawn upon on top of a larger sheet of paper or newspaper and have them make an image as large as possible. When the picture is finished and lifted off of the larger bottom sheet, the picture has gone "Over the Edge."

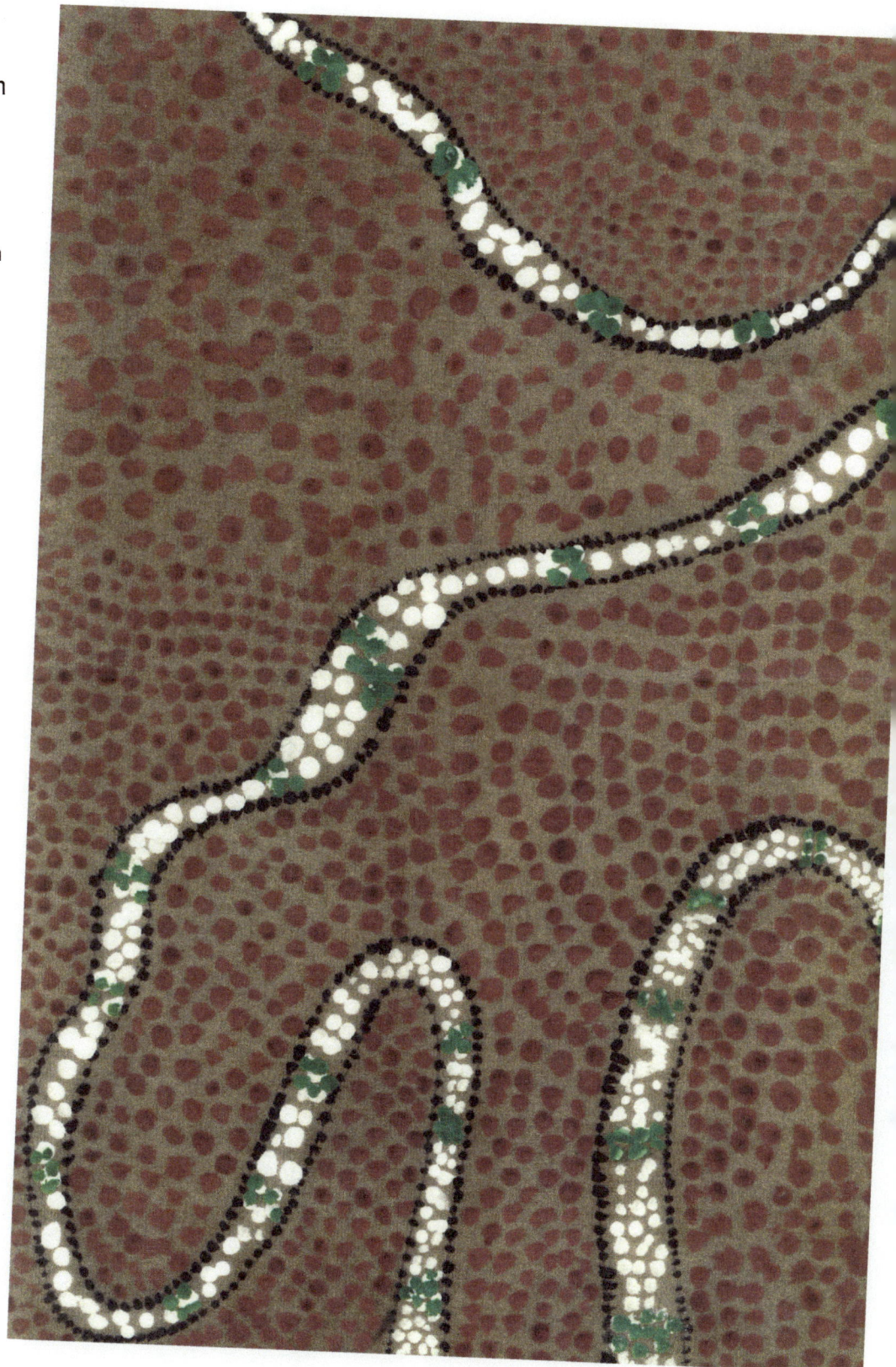

Snake
Aborigine inspired art – 5th Grade

Rule #1

Make It As Big As You Can Art and Reading

"Make the subject as big as you can." and "Make something happen in your picture." Simply looking at a picture gives us much more information. Pictures give us adjectives and adverbs. Our brain views art directly and immediately. Reading takes a moment and must be in an alphabet we can understand.

We see pictures before we can attach meaning to sounds and configurations. The ancient Egyptian phonetic alphabet was depicted in pictures.

Rule #1

Make It As Big As You Can **Cropping**

There are two ways to fill up a space: enlarge the image within the frame (the edges of your paper are your "frame") or shrink the frame to make the image appear bigger.

TRY:

Take one fragment of a picture and make it "monumental."

Cut windows 11/2" X 2" and move over picture to find an interesting section. Then crop to include just that view.

Uneven is more interesting that even.

Over the edge—Impact at a distance

Scale—Outlines/Edge Lines

Examples from a third grade class.

Rule #1

Make It As Big As You Can **Color it all in**

To help a child carefully "color it all in", sit with a child and color along with them. Color untouched areas so they can see the difference solid color makes.

Divide a picture in half and color just one side, leaving the other side just as they did it. Children will be amazed at the difference.

Backgrounds are often an extension of the "color it all in" rule.

Coloring the sky as a blue strip across the top of the paper and the earth as a strip across the bottom typical for most children. They do this in child art all over the world. Children see the sky above their heads so it must be "up" on their paper and know that the Earth is below. It's part of the developmental transference from reality to depiction on a flat surface.

We can help a child see that color is everywhere and how it makes their pictures so much prettier. Unless this is pointed out to them, children will continue coloring the sky as a simple strip across the top of their paper as late as 3rd grade.

Rule #2

Color It All In The Color Wheel / Chart

Color can occupy an artist for a lifetime. It is closely allied with the study of light. Visual Literacy looks at color as a tool. It only asks, "How can I use color to achieve the effect I want?"

Understanding color opposites comes as children understand verbal opposites: up, down; in, out. Foreground and background fall into the same simplistic category of opposites.

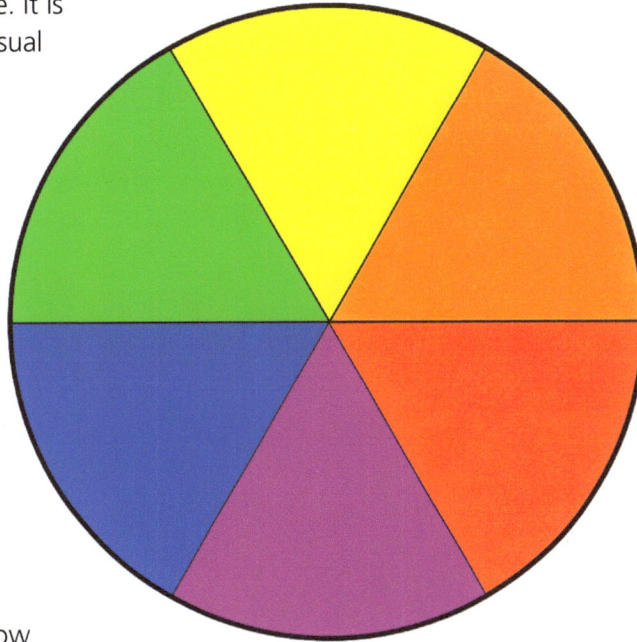

The use of a simple six-color color wheel with the three primary colors of blue, yellow and red and their three "complimentary colors" of orange, purple and green, which are called "secondary colors", can be helpful in engaging a child's imagination with scientific understanding. Secondary colors are created by adding two primary colors. Red mixed with yellow makes orange. Blue mixed with red makes purple. Yellow mixed with blue makes green. The complimentary color of another color is found directly opposite on the color wheel.

The complete spectrum of colors is immeasurable, of course. But for the child, the six-color wheel is enough information.

Color in our visual language equates to adjectives and adverbs in our verbal language.

The subtlety of using white as a color comes as students get away from relying on all white backgrounds and start seeing in color blocks. This typically doesn't begin to happen until the upper grades or with more advanced students.

Too much technical talk about value scales, color theory, illumination, intensity and hue can overload students 7-14 years of age.

Rule #2

Color It All In Light

Light is the essence of art and photography. Artists and professional photographers spend their lifetimes fascinated by light and attempting to capture the effects of light.

Expressing light requires contrast, angles, and shadows. To adequately study light in a classroom, a single strong light source is typically needed.

Lighting instruction seems to work best with students when we point out the highest contrasts. Focusing on the darkest darks and lightest lights while working on a mid toned surface can simplify this process for them more easily.

Rule #2
Color It All In **Shadows**

Make shadows using different colors, different shapes, and in different locations.

Shadows are: attached, a similar shape, a mirror image, on the opposite side of the light source, and become lighter as they move away from the object they are attached to.

Children can be taught shadows as early as kindergarten. Shadows are easiest to learn in high contrast black and white situations. This requires a strong directional light source.

At first attempt, don't have students make a picture with shadows by relying on their memory or imagination alone. Help them to look and see without making an assumption. Then encourage their imagination with the use of shadows. Have them draw a realistic object with a shadow using a strong light source and let their imagination go free.

Original drawing 2nd Grade
Non-sense drawing.

Rule #2
Color It All In Special Effects

Side Lighting: Main light source is from the side.

Straight On: Light source is pointed directly at the subject.

Over Head: Light source is directly over the subject.

Northern Exposure: This refers to the north facing direction of windows or sky lights in artist's loft or studio. With a northern exposure artists are assured soft steady light and are able to work for longer periods of time.

Chiaroscuro: An Italian term, it is the interplay between light and shadow often seen in the late afternoons or after storms.

Golden Hour: It is the hour just after sunrise and the hour before sunset. The angled light has a quality not available at any other time of the day, producing long shadows. Ansel Adams knew this and got up early to photograph his images of Yosemite Valley, to capture those Golden Hour results.

Artists and photographers constantly search for geographical locations noted for the quality of the sun's light.

Rule #2
Color It All In **Silhouettes**

Everybody loves silhouettes. Parents treasure them. They naturally evolve as imaginations develop, from profiles to hand shadows to negative space images.

Silhouette technique is a natural way to work with the science of light. The profile silhouette can follow the same process as the phases of the moon. By moving the light source, the child can witness a change in the shape of their silhouette.

Rule #3

Make Something Happen In Your Picture **Uneven Is More Interesting than Even**

Uneven is more interesting than even. There are several ways to teach this.

Uneven numbers: As soon as children learn to count by 2's and know the difference between even and uneven numbers, they actually enjoy counting the number of objects in their pictures.

For some reason, three is the most satisfying number there is. Three of anything automatically gives an interesting composition. Five also works. But we don't need to bother counting numbers above seven to see if they are even or uneven.

Make an image come alive:

Asymmetrical is more fascinating than symmetrical.

Rule #3

Make Something Happen In Your Picture In's and Out's

Saying that something has lots of in's and out's is the short, easy way to refer to uneven edge lines. Kindergartners and first graders easily catch hold of the phrase and concept.

In's and out's applied to the edge lines or outlines of a subject are dramatically obvious when using negative space, outlining with wide lines or using outrageous color.

A picture's in's and out's adds rhythm and movement, making something happen in your picture. It is a key element in giving the simplest picture visual energy.

In's and out's give the eyes something to latch onto. With beginning reading, it helps to outline the word so the child actually reads the word shape.

Word shape is why signs on the interstate highways are printed in lower case letters rather than all caps. Travelers can easily read the word shape in a second.

Students often need practice in cutting freehand shapes with exaggerated flowing shapes.

This was done after studying Matisse's "Cut Outs". 2nd grade

Rule #3

Make Something Happen In Your Picture **Viewpoints**

The ability to see things from different angles to adopt various points of view is crucial to art innovation.

First grade is not too early to begin seeing things from different angles. We can begin with choosing a subject. A bunny, for example. Make a picture of just the bunny all by itself. Now, what if we walked around to the other side of the bunny? Make another picture. How does the bunny look
from the back, the front and the top?

Search for different views both with and without viewfinders, real or imagined, laying on backs, stomachs, under things, in corners, looking up, down.

Paint or draw pictures on a block of wood, showing all six sides of the subject, or draw each view into a different section of folded paper. SIX views!

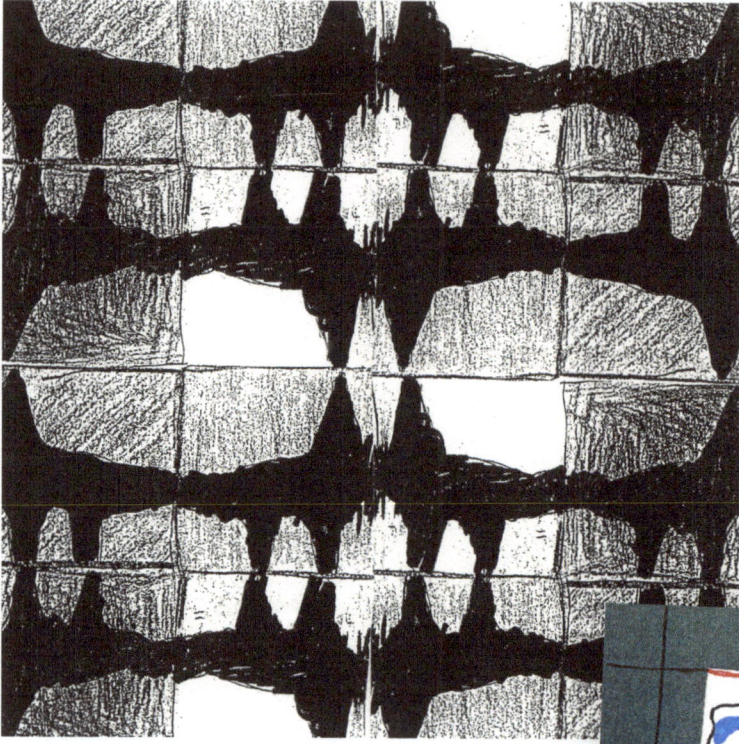

Level 2

Elements of Visual Literacy

Seeing patterns in nature and seeing natural movement are keys in seeing structure in science, mathematics, physics, linguistics, and art.

There are two types of patterns: the pattern within the art motif itself, and the pattern made by repeating the design. Art helps identify natural patterns.

Level 2

Elements of Visual Literacy Patterns of Nature

The basic Patterns of Nature wonderfully correspond to the five basic elements of art:

Line

Circle

Triangle

Wave

Spiral

Teaching from the patterns of nature allows infinite possibilities across all disciplines. Both science and art spring from a base of acute pattern recognition-- the comfort level of Visual Literacy.

Line: Line corresponds to the basic physics of starting and stopping. Nature seldom draws in straight lines except in crystalline forms. Life prefers curves. In geometry, lines intersect producing exquisite patterns. Through art, we connect with living and non-living lines, thick, thin, straight and curved.

Circle: A closed line segment, along with the triangle, it is the most satisfying visual shape no matter round, elliptical or egg. Look for it in the natural world as an explosion, radiation, starfish, sea urchin, flower, and dandelion.

Triangle: The triangle is the third pattern found in nature, corresponding to balance in physics. The triangle defines both consolidation and flowing geometric balance. Its line intersections are a study in mathematics and philosophy. The closed line pyramid is our most satisfying earth-connected shape.

Wave: The wave is one of our earliest motifs. It is basic to communication and the transfer of information. Waves, such as light, travel forever until they strike a receptor. Wave patterns are found in meandering rivers, ripples and waves, snakes, sand dunes, and ridges on shells.

Spiral: The spiral is the design of life itself. The chambered nautilus, pinecones, sunflower seed patterns, roses unfolding, all illustrate this impulse of Nature to sublimely pattern itself.

Level 2

Elements of Visual Literacy **Lines**

Physics motion: Starting, stopping

The rudiments of art are thought to be line, space and color. Here are a few explorations to try with art lines:

Art made of stripes

Time lines

Drawing a complete image with just 1 line

Charting strategy

Mobius strips

Morse code patterns

Level 2

Elements of Visual Literacy **Lines**

Lines interact in predictable ways. They can be straight, curved, meandering, horizontal, and vertical, as well as all degrees in between. We need to know this for science and we need to know this for art.

Parallel lines remain parallel whether they are straight, curved, or intertwined; whether they are tubular or lanes on the Interstate. Young students can remember the word "parallel" because the l's in it are parallel.

Intersecting lines in nature seldom meet at right angles, except in crystalline and metallic forms. All other biological forms intersect at diagonal angles.

Curved lines are at the aesthetic and engineering zenith. The Roman aqueducts stand as one of civilization's breakthroughs and structures of enduring beauty.

Recognizing types of lines and how they form patterns connects art, science, mathematics, and engineering.

Preschool

Level 2

Elements of Visual Literacy **Vertical Lines**

Students get their bearings from the vertical and horizontal edges of their papers in the same way that they do from the walls, ceiling, and floor of their room.

Vertical lines in the center, whether they are actual or insinuated, will divide a picture in half and automatically call for a formal or symmetrical composition. If strong vertical lines are moved over to one side, the composition will become asymmetrical or informal. It becomes an uneven composition and "Uneven is more interesting than even."

When drawing vertical lines, encourage starting the line at the top and pulling the line in towards the body. There is better muscular control pulling arms in to the body than away from it.

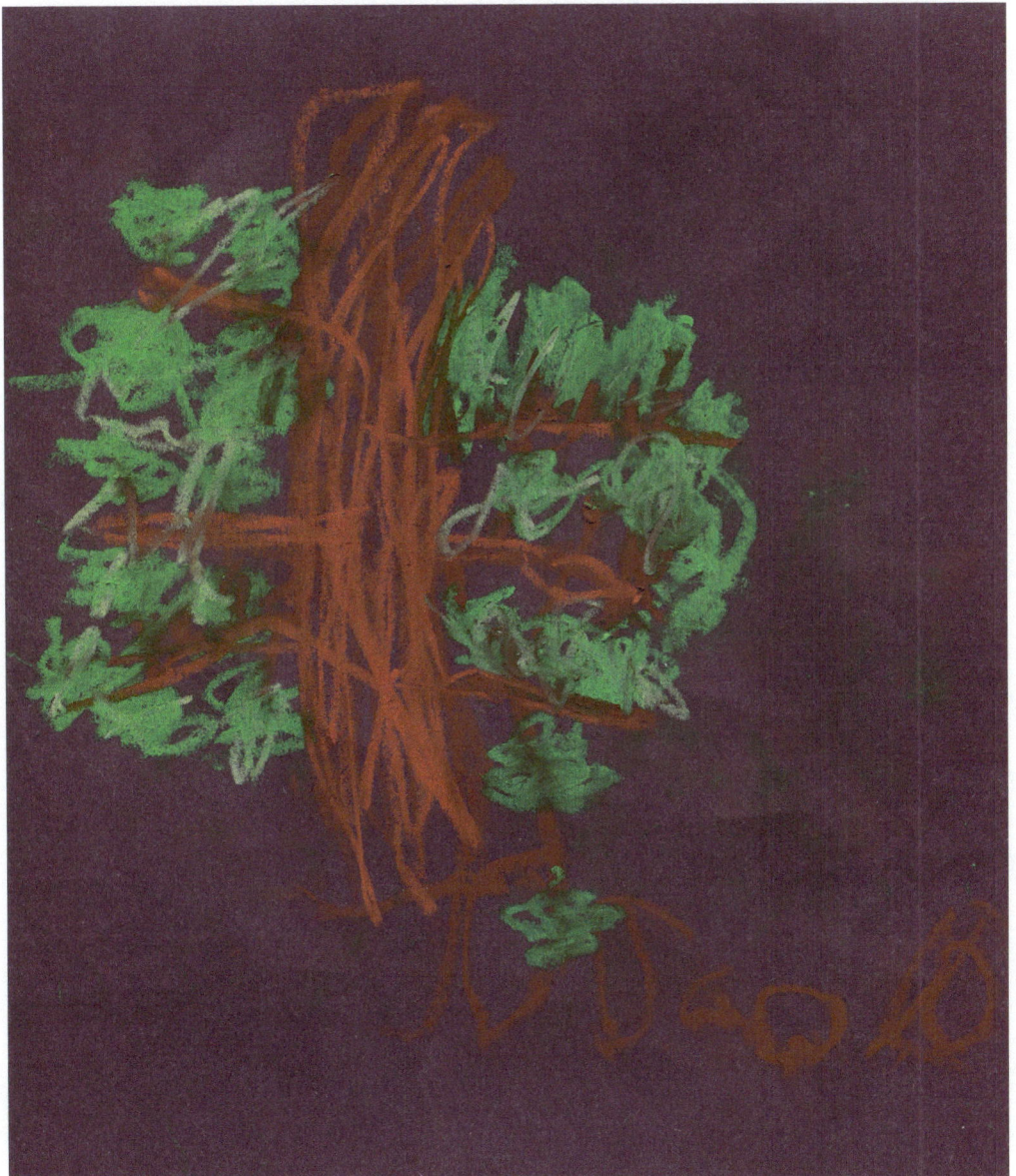

6 year old - First week of first grade

Level 2

Elements of Visual Literacy **Horizontal Lines**

Horizontal lines are strong elements of composition. Taken from the root word, horizon, they are stabilizing forces in any composition. Used as a distant horizon, horizon lines are restful to the eyes and mind. They are the first line a child draws before adding the sky "above", and the sun in the corner. They are easy to live with, especially when they are repeated, as often happens in landscapes where there often is a horizontal line of trees or horizontal edge lines of a lake or hill.

The position of a horizontal line defines the division of space in a picture. They are strong, especially when they are straight across the picture. They can effectively stop the visual flow within the picture. If the line can be made uneven, even slightly diagonal, it will resume the flow.

Students also have the tendency, when they hear the words "straight" and "line", to pull out their rulers. It's an automatic response. But unless they are actually measuring something precise, rulers are best left in desks.

Level 2

Elements of Visual Literacy Diagonal Lines

This is the strongest of all action lines. Our eyes have been trained, through reading, to go from left to right, zig-zag back to the left, and then go to the right again. We continue this same pattern when we look at all of our visual images. In a brochure, poster, or flyer, our eyes travel this pattern.

Converging Diagonals

If a diagonal is the most captivating of lines, imagine how engaged a viewer is with two diagonals. These are called converging diagonals. Looking like a tipsy L, it can go in any direction.

Level 2

Elements of Visual Literacy Eye-Lines

Eye lines are the most influential of all lines. Eye-lines found in Visual Literacy are the invisible, imagined lines that go from a person's (or animals) eyes toward someone or something. It can be either in or out of the picture's frame. Our eyes will automatically follow the line.

Mona Lisa

Level 2

Elements of Visual Literacy Width Variation

Line width is a potent part of Visual Literacy.

Variation in line widths adds subtle interest because while we accept the value and direction of lines toward building the shapes that make up a picture, such as edge lines or outlines, line width itself is subliminal.

Outlining with a fine black line makes an elegant statement. A fine black outline defines the object without calling attention to itself. An example of this is the fine black line around a printed photograph accenting the photo without being noticed.

Children who are drawing with outlines might try colored crayons or chalk, even twisting the crayon as they draw, rather than using pencil. Big crayons make a bold statement, giving more variety of width and less control. Variation in line width adds interest. "Uneven is more interesting than even." It's an extension of our Rule #2: Make something happen in your picture."

Level 2

Elements of Visual Literacy **Lead-In Lines**

Lead-in lines are a basic structure of Visual Literacy. These are the lines that lead our eyes away from the edge of a picture back again to the center of interest. They precisely pin-point the focal point. These are edge lines of objects, shapes, colors or shadows that "make something happen" in our pictures. First, we need to identify the subject, or focal point, of our picture. Next, we have to know what edge lines are and be able to recognize and follow them.

In the upper elementary grades there is a big leap in recognizing the subtleties of lead-in lines. By then, students seem to be comfortable with all other kinds of lines and are able to interconnect and follow them.

Level 2

Elements of Visual Literacy Pointillism: Drawing Without Lines

An astounding advancement in perception was made by the French Pointillists who used tiny points of color, overlapping them to create color illustrations.

Drawing without lines is a patient, absorbing technique that actually works as early as second grade. Children become fascinated dipping all those little dots.

This technique is more obvious when using only black markers. Shading is produced by the density of dots. Areas flow into each other and the images appear only at a distance. Refer to art history with the study of Seurat, Monet, pointillism, the Impressionists, and studies of mosaics in Pompeii and Rome.

Level 2

Elements of Visual Literacy Gesture Drawing/Unbroken Lines

Gesture drawings are fast line drawings that capture the basic shape and movement of a subject.

Try having a student gesture wildly in all directions and call "FREEZE!" The rest of the class then has to try and capture the movement on paper in just a few seconds, without lifting the hand to the count of 1-2-3-STOP!

OR, do the opposite. Go very slowly, consciously, deliberately, anticipating each move.

Draw an unbroken line drawing self-portrait: drawn while looking in the mirror but without looking at the paper. 5th grade

A gesture must be drawn quickly, using line width effectively, and evoking just the essence of the subject. Tape down a sheet of paper so it won't move. A variety of mediums can be tried: chalk, pastel, conte' crayon, charcoal, ink brush, or water color. Try it with the opposite hand.

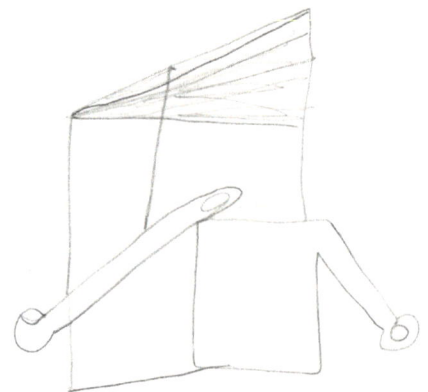

Level 2

Elements of Visual Literacy Symmetry

Symmetry in art correlates to balance within the realm of science.

Kids love learning the term "symmetrical." It's not too big to say, it can be introduced as early as first grade using ink blots to make butterflies, mirror images, reflections in water or whatever else the student can imagine.

"Symmetrical" gives the mathematical connotation of being exactly equal. This means that whatever is on one side of the centerline is exactly, quantitatively, the same as what is on the other side. Artists use a looser term: formal.

A formal composition is not so precise as a mathematical one. It is balanced but not measurably so. We are attracted to formal compositions through their subject matter, the skill or technique of the artist and their calming sameness. Artists make formal compositions interesting by breaking out in vibrant, unanticipated colors and using oversize shapes.

Level 2

Elements of Visual Literacy **Focal Point**

The focal point in a picture is very specific. It is the point at which our eyes focus after being irresistibly drawn through the maze of lead-in lines. It is a stage production of composition lines. It uses the more technical elements of Visual Literacy so finding focal points is better suited to the upper grades.

Every picture that uses standard composition has a focal point. Modern artists, however, often omit focal points as a way to engage the viewer.

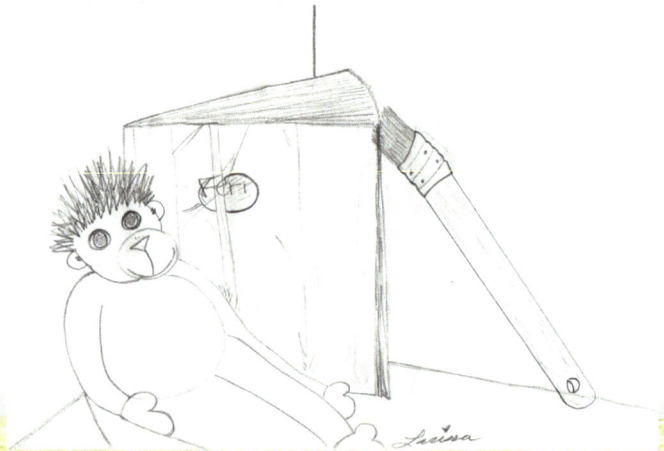

Level 2

Elements of Visual Literacy Balance/Weight

Here are five basic "rules" of balance/weight.

1. The primary optical area is the upper left-hand corner, because that is where we have been trained to start reading.

2. Large areas are noticed more, seen for a longer time, and remembered better than small areas.

3. High contrasting color areas carry more optical weight than low contrasting areas.

4. Color conveys more optical weight than black and white areas.

5. White space, or "empty" space, serves to draw viewer's attention to whatever is in the "non-empty" space.

Level 2

Elements of Visual Literacy Triangle

Nature constantly seeks gravitational balance. A tripod, a pendulum in motion, balance scales, levers, pulleys all work on this 3-point balancing act.

What else is a triangle?
A mountain?
A sitting Teddy Bear?
The pyramids?

We can get the feel of the stability of the pyramid shape by making folded paper animals, and the balance inherent in the triangle by making mobiles.

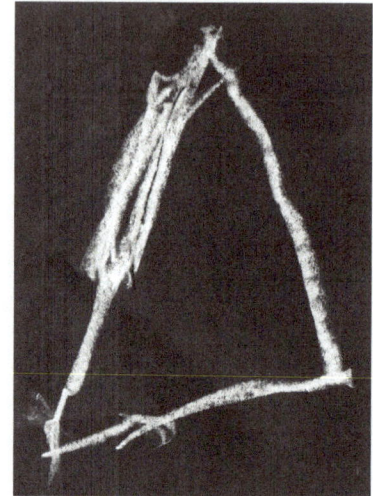

Level 2

Elements of Visual Literacy **Proportions**

When children try to draw realistically, their proportions are usually "off".

Proportions are the relationship of one part to another. What is the actual visual relationship?

There are several ways to approach proportions, and we can start as young as third grade:

1. Studying head and facial proportions to become aware that there is such a thing as proportion or relationship. Self-portraits are a good place to start, using a large mirror, even putting tape over the mirror for emphasis.

2. Cartooning is a great way to emphasize and legitimize wrong proportions.

3. The Artist Pencil Trick: The old cliché of artists holding their thumbs or pencils up at arms length to measure visual proportions between the pencil end and the thumb nail really does work. It's a fun class practice!

4. We can also learn how to change scale. Choose or draw a picture. Divide it into graph sections (squares are easiest). Re-draw the picture in a larger graphed area. Or, reverse the process and draw it on a smaller scale.

Level 2

Elements of Visual Literacy Cartooning

Invariably people will draw faces with the subject facing front, which is actually the most difficult direction.

One way to avoid the frontal facial trap is through cartooning. We can learn a lot by copying cartooning technique. Cartooning is produced by deliberately distorting proportions. Eyes or mouths that are too big, chins that are too small, hair that stands up straight, these are all signatures of cartooning.

MonA LISA

Larissa B.

Level 2

Elements of Visual Literacy **Enlarging/Reducing/Distorting**

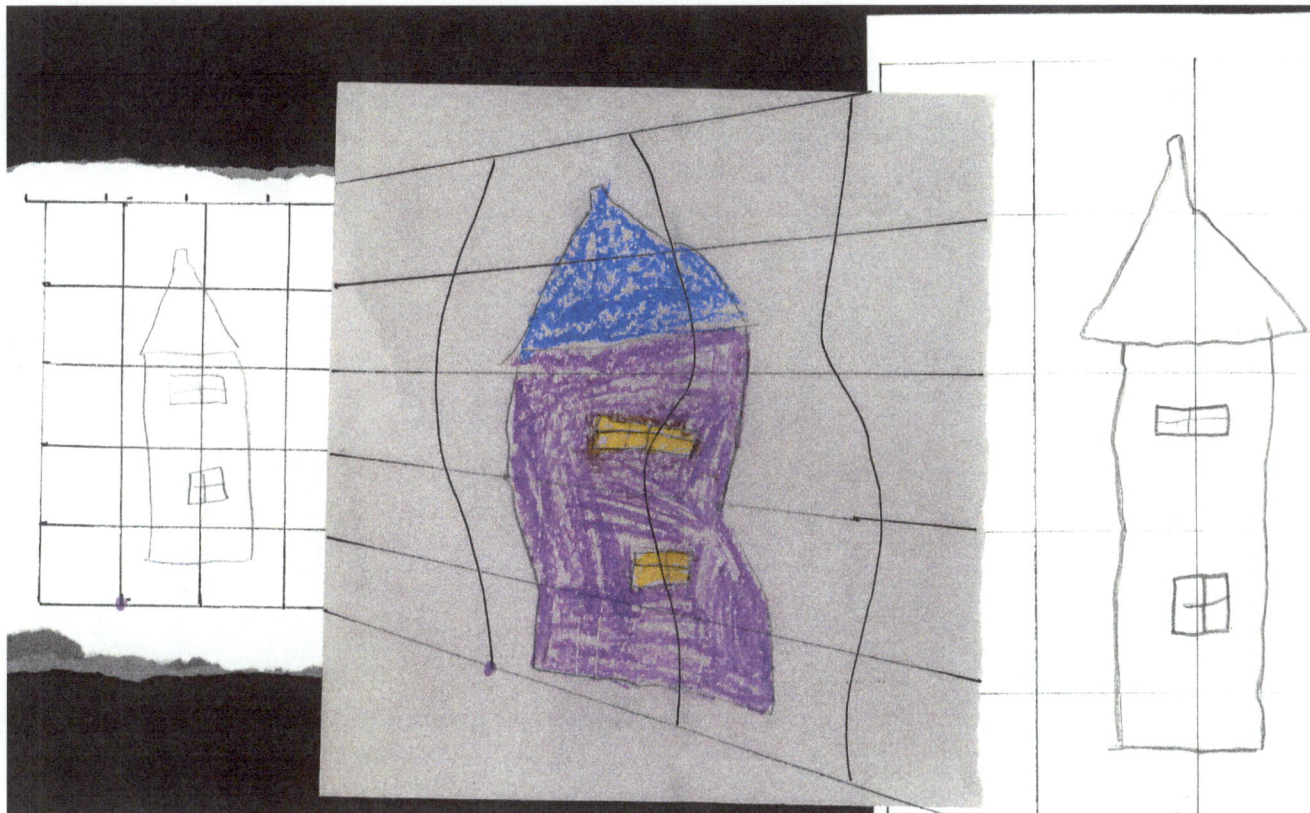

Enlarging and reducing using the grid system is a skill we all need to know. Even though this is easily done on copiers, cameras and computers, there is always a situation where we need to be able to do this manually. It's like being glad we learned our times tables when we can't find our calculator.

It is also an excellent way to practice the skill of finding relative points of edge lines and accurate measuring. Grid enlarging uses the same skill as drawing through a viewfinder.

Exactly measure and draw into an equal number of squares the picture to be enlarged or reduced and its corresponding empty area. Copy the picture in each square, noticing where the edge lines of the image touch the edges of the squares.

Distortion, on the other hand, flips the brain over to the right side. It tries to make sense where, obviously, no sense appears.

Level 2

Elements of Visual Literacy Spirals/Waves/Repetition/Rhythm

In mathematics, a spiral is a curve, which emanates from a central point, getting progressively farther away as it revolves around the point.

"Mathematics, rightly viewed, possesses not only truth, but supreme beauty … such as only the greatest art can show." – Bertrand Russell

Rhythm in art, like rhythm in music, works best when it is felt.

Repeated patterns are easy for kids of all ages to identify and sink their teeth into. They're like drum beats. Repeated patterns, or repetition, always produce pleasing, even striking results. An easy way to get the feel of rhythm is by using simple words like "repeat" "over again" "some more" and tapping out the rhythm while pointing to each time the pattern is repeated.

Spiral with line drawings - 5th Grade.

Repeated patterns while studying a frog - 4th grade.

Level 2

Elements of Visual Literacy **Branching/Fractals**

The mathematics behind fractals began to take shape in the 17th century. Branching patterns can be observed in trees, river deltas, erosion patterns and wherever water flows. We see it also in lightning.

This natural branching pattern can be used to make beautiful tree pictures simply by chasing a splash of paint across a sheet of paper with a straw. Try 2 color fractals.

Try adding tissue paper blossoms or torn paper colored leaves for autumn pictures.

Fractals: blown Tempera paint tree outline, marker background, sponge painting --Shandi Wagner, 3rd Grade

Level 2

Elements of Visual Literacy Tessellation

Tessellations are seen throughout art history, from ancient architecture to modern art. Identical objects, they meet in groups of 3 at 120-degree angles.

Cracking patterns become more complex, but they still follow fixed laws. While cracking patterns generally follow the 120-degree 3-way split, at intersections where stress is greatest, right-angle splits may form.

This 3-way packing pattern can be creatively rendered through patterns of tessellation, or decoration with a mosaic effect. Fourth graders can start handling this, but fifth graders do better. These are beautiful, intellectually satisfying, comprehensive designs.

Level 2

Elements of Visual Literacy **Charts/Vectors/Graphs/Maps**

Creating graphs and charts, beyond the predictability of computer-generated visuals, is a skill and an art.

There are pie charts, horizontal bar charts, vertical bar charts, and fever charts. This form of Visual Literacy should be included in every grade and all subjects, beginning in first grade, with horizontal bar charts and discovery maps.

Designing charts and graphs are real mind stretchers, especially diagrams. It has been stated that maps, charts, and graphs require measurement, comparison, analysis, and coming to a conclusion, all receiving current learning emphasis. This information can be compiled with computer graphics.

A vector graphics is the use of points, lines, curves, and shapes or polygon(s), which are all based on mathematical equations, to represent images in computer graphics.

Level 2

Elements of Visual Literacy **Circles/Rotation/Logos/Icons**

Circles, Rotation

One of the primary design motifs of nature; the visual impact of the circle is seen as inseparable from the physical motion of spinning.

Circular design elements are present as ovals and loops, radiation, explosions, and splashes. Its 2-D rendering is seen in kiwi fruit seed patterns, dandelions, bubbles, circuitry, and orbits. The applications of circular motion extend from interstellar space to wind-up clocks.

Starbursts

Children the world over will put a sun in their picture up until around third grade, the developmental stage equivalent to the Renaissance on the "Expanding Pathway." They will also automatically use radiation lines to signify the energy lines, even though they are invisible to the naked eye.

Logos and Icons

Logos and computer icons are tight informational designs that must be instantly recognizable, their meaning clear and unambiguous.

Icons are computer-instigated art in a genre advancing as technology advances. Logos, however, have been around since the craft guilds of the Renaissance. Before that, there were the family coats of arms of the Dark Ages. Both logos and icons were flat, lack detail, are simple, even cartoon like. They use either no shading three shades of gray: light, medium and dark. There is little or no background.

One idea that works is to study the icons on computers as well as company logos on cereal boxes to create personal logos or icons.

Level 2

Elements of Visual Literacy Composition

H

Composition is a structure of lines of energy. The energy flow is present even without a well-defined imprint or recognizable shape. Certain compositions form letters whose familiar shapes are pleasing to the eye.

When first looking at this composition, "H" gives the appearance of being stiff and formal. But it can be bent and curved to give very graceful lines. Learning to see structure within a picture is what Visual Literacy is all about.

Because an "H" composition is basically formal, it gives a pleasing, sensible balance to a picture. But let's take a look at what can be done with it. Try the following techniques:

> Curve the lines
>
> Give the lines different weights
>
> Raise or lower the cross bar

Then ask yourself, "is the basic "H" composition recognizable?

L

This is a composition that always works. It's made up of converging diagonal lines. The trick is to be able to visualize the "L" in all kinds of positions, of seeing it at different angles.

These angels could be formed or defined by edge lines, shadows, subject areas, or color blocks. There is an automatic balance between the L-shaped areas and the background or negative-space areas.

The subject or focal point naturally snuggles into the corner of the L, so the lead-in lines direct the eye to it. They can't miss.

Now, look again. The invisible or understood closure line forms a triangle, the geometry of balance. This composition is psychologically pleasing no matter how you look at it.

Level 2

Elements of Visual Literacy The Rule of Thirds

The fascination with dividing space into areas goes as far back as Pythagoras, an early Greek mathematician and philosopher. He not only divided space up into areas, he also divided sound up into areas. These sound divisions are the basis for our scales and octaves. With both of these divisions, sound and space, uneven is generally more interesting than even.

Amazingly, what Pythagoras discovered still governs our sound and visual divisions. Dividing space can be remembered by the general 1/3 rule. Our horizon line will be more pleasing if we put it across the upper or lower third of our picture rather than in the middle.

Our subject placement will always be agreeable if we place it at the intersections of thirds in our picture. Learning to "see" this probably comes easiest by looking at a whole picture first and discovering the divisions within it, which is probably how Pythagoras did it in the first place. Using large format art prints works great here.

While studying Piet Mondrian in connection with division of space - 5th Grade

Level 2

Elements of Visual Literacy Concept/Technique/Subject/Imagination

This Christmas card was created with chalk and watercolor in the ancient Egyptian style. Notice that the heads are turned sideways and there is slight overlapping.

Level 2

Elements of Visual Literacy Scribble Pictures

Scribble pictures usually have no focal point.

There are three stages in scribble perception, following the same unconscious sequence as our developmental sequence.

Stage 1: At first children just color in the sections with random colors. Older children can use this technique to sharpen their concept of color and value.

Stage 2: Color in little pictures within the loops.

Stage 3: Find one large image from the entire scribble. This is learning to expand awareness of the bigger picture. Add lines to the scribble that are needed and color over lines that are not needed. Visualize forms suggested by the lines rather than impose a pre-conceived form.

Try doing this with your opposite or non-dominant hand, doing this with both hands, and doing it with music.

Level 3

Visual Space Flat Art

Flat painting has neither form nor shading. There is no depth.

Modern artists may adopt a flat painting style, like Matisse. Much contemporary Native American painting is also done with a flat technique.

Drawn outline with inside patterns - Kindergarten.

Drawn outline with inside patterns - Kindergarten.

Level 3

Visual Space **Negative Space**

Here is an example from a third grade girl who, after cutting out a random shape from white paper, exclaimed, "Oh, I have a kitty!" Then she added the eyes and claws.

The negative space in a page layout is often called white space. White space is the blank space between pictures, type and margins.

M.C.Escher visited the Alhambra, a Moorish fortress in Spain, in 1936 and was struck by the reverse imaging of the intricate tiles. He then began years of reverse imagining and tessellation.

Recognizing empty or negative space in a picture is like discovering the meaning of "zero" in mathematics or making the connection between letters and sounds--we suddenly advance to another level of understanding.

Using high contrast is one point of entry into seeing this phenomenon. Stark black and white is most common because of the high contrast.

Here is an example from a third grade girl who, after cutting out a random shape from white paper, exclaimed, "Oh, I have a kitty!" Then she added the eyes and claws.

Level 3

Visual Space **All-Over Patterns**

In an all-over design, we can paraphrase Gertrude Stein's "A rose is a rose is a rose" and say, "A subject is a subject is a subject." With all-over design, there is no focal point and the subject is repeated randomly.

An all-over design is like flopping down into a field of wildflowers. We are completely surrounded. We have to entertain a certain amount of abandon to replicate the random order of nature and lose ourselves in a fragrant bouquet of lilacs.

All-over designs can be approached two ways: through overlapping wildly as in replicating nature, or by the orderly progression of patterns to ever more complex designs as in fractal geometry and networking, the science of our connected age.

All-over patterns are seldom found spontaneously in children's art.

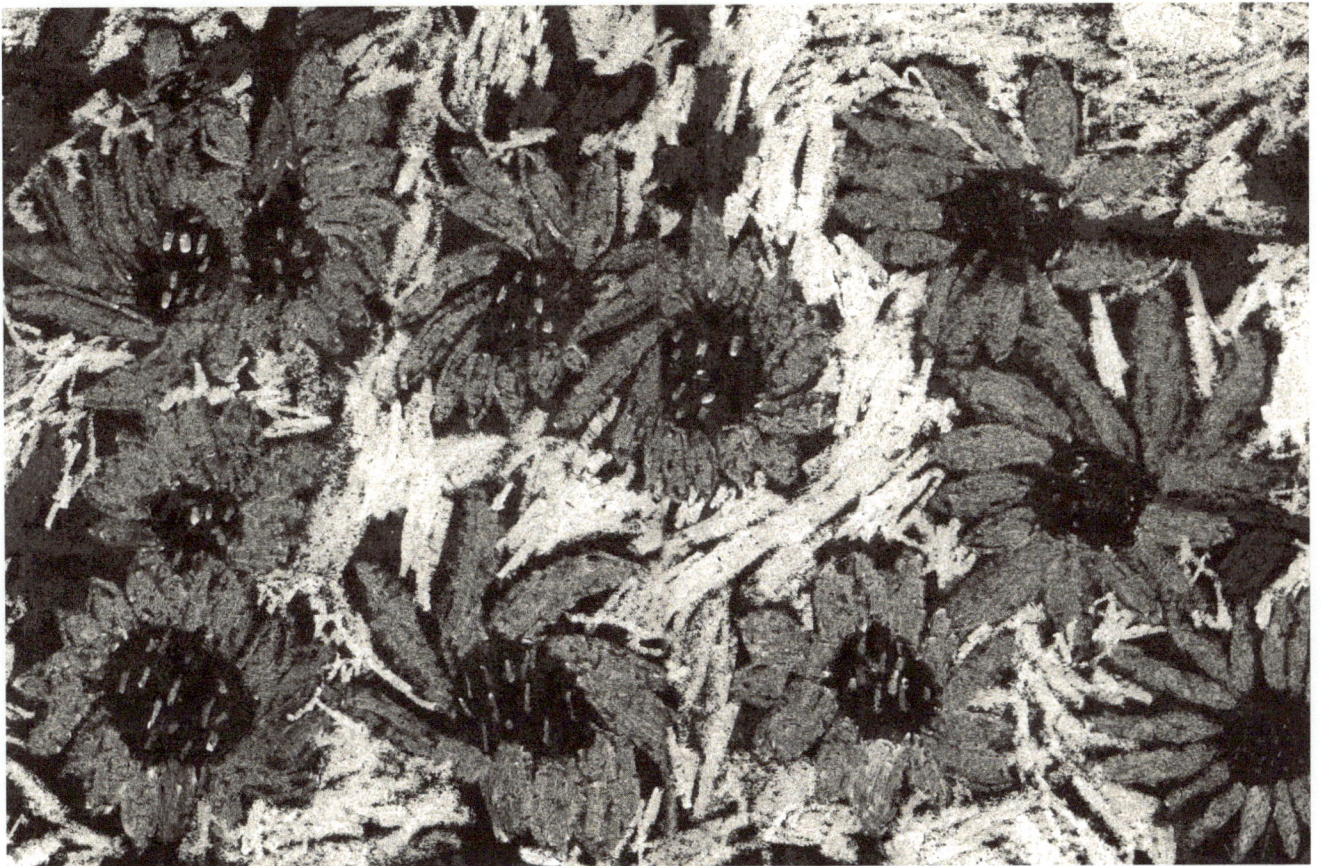

Third Grade

Level 3

Visual Space Edge Lines

The first step beyond stick figures is drawing the outside edge of figures then coloring inside the lines coloring book style. Children recognize the term "outline" as early as first grade and can have fun outlining in surprising colors, making outlines both thick and thin.

Students can start recognizing edge lines as early as second grade. More subtle than outlines, they define edges between color or texture changes or stark graphic lines.

Edge lines morph into contour lines or contour drawing. Contour drawing describes any line, inside as well as outside, dividing colors, shades, or textures. Awareness of edge lines is vital when copying a picture that is up-side down, forcing the brain into right brain mode.

Recognizing edge lines is important. Spotting where they enter and exit picture frames is used when graphing enlargements and in section-by-section cooperative painting. In the example below, a picture is cut into smaller equal sections without the student seeing the whole picture until it is completed and re-assembled. Students execute each section using whatever materials and technique they choose, being especially careful with noticing the placement of entering and exiting edge lines. The end result: the pieces fit together as one unit. These sectioned paintings turn into amazing wall-sized pictures.

Level 3

Visual Space **Depth**

Distance: Size

"Near is big; far is small."

Young children grasp the opposites of big and little, large and small, here and there, near and far. They understand these comparisons, but applying the concept to create distance in pictures is still another developmental step.

Second graders can start putting the concepts together of "Near is big; far is small." Start by introducing them in isolation. Near and far. Big and small. These are the easiest depth comparisons to make.

Discovering and utilizing depth and distance into a flat surface is another way of discovering space. It helps if students are comfortable with two contrasting elements of depth or distance before tackling three.

All students can begin by making contrasting pictures. They can even cut out big and little images, comparing them separately like, "Which is bigger?" "Which one is nearer or closer?" "Which one is farther?" "How do we know?' "Which is the closest?"

There is an opposite application that can be given to older students. This is used more often with imaginative art to give the illusion of depth. It is very dramatic. This time, make the smaller images in the foreground and the bigger images in the background. The eyes will get drawn into the picture and go directly to the larger images in the background making them more important. The color rules add special effect.

1st Grade

Level 3

Visual Space Overlapping/Layering

Overlapping means that one object is overlapping another. One is on top, and one or more is underneath. It is one of the benchmarks connecting children's art to the Bigger Picture and fits squarely in second or third grade.

An easy beginning rule is: "When you come to another line, stop. Then pick it up on the other side."

Uncertainty with overlapping is normal with young children . 2nd Grade

Level 3

Visual Space Foreground/Mid-ground/Background

"Near is sharp; far is fuzzy."

When it comes to transferring distance/depth to a flat surface, Renaissance artists made quantum leaps in perception.

"Near is sharp; far is fuzzy." This is the last of the depth or distance rules and the hardest to do. It is definitely third grade and up, probably best at fifth grade.

This rule works best with various brush and chalk techniques that can be smudged on the background or horizon line. It's a little more advanced than the other distance rules and allowances should be made when trying to do it. It takes time to execute the difference between a smudge and a mess.

Practice seeing this in the paintings of skilled artists. How did they do it? Start with the Renaissance and go right on up to skilled current illustrators.

Level 3

Visual Space Color/Focus

One way to emphasize foreground brightness is to make foreground images on white paper in vivid colors, cut them out and paste them on grayed construction paper as the grayed background. Distant images can be added on the gray paper using pencil, charcoal, black markers, or gray crayon. You can also have students observe and conclude what bright against gray does, using color samples.

"Near is bright; far is gray."

As when learning all new concepts, grasping the idea of distance builds on understanding the simpler ideas first and then expanding from there. It's easier to start with two contrasting distance elements and then expanding into the three distance elements of foreground, mid-ground, and background.

Besides focus, placement, and size, what else can artists do to make things look farther away? They can use color. Third grade is a good time to start working with graying distance colors.

"Near is bright; far is gray."

This is easy to say, but, as always, life is not that simple. Applying this phrase to our pictures is dependent upon:

Recognizing what is near and what is far

Recognizing the difference between bright and grayed colors

Being familiar with the color wheel

Knowing how to mix grayed colors

Colors are grayed by mixing with their color opposites

Knowing the positions of the primary and secondary colors and being able to locate their opposites or color complements

Understanding "warm" and "cool" colors, which can also be used

Visual Space **Placement**

Near is low. Far is high.

There seems to be a natural tendency for children to do this when making a landscape because they are duplicating their normal field of vision. This childlike idea of distance has ruled Oriental and Persian paintings.

Objects that are closer to us in the picture frame appear lower and things that appear farther away are placed higher. This works as a distance factor when the other distance rules, such as size, color, and focus, are also followed. A tree in the distance would not just be placed higher, it would also be smaller, grayer, and fuzzier.

Level 3

Visual Space **1-Point Perspective**

This is the first more technical solution to showing distance or depth in a picture.

When introduced to one-point perspective, students start by describing what they see as being "bigger at the bottom and smaller at the top." The term "disappearing point" seems to be easier to recall than the term "perspective". Before beginning, a few math concepts are needed such as:

      Horizon line
      Parallel
      Intersecting points
      Diagonal
      Vertical

Ideally, students would need T-squares and triangles in order to get true horizontal and vertical lines. However, a ruler will do. Free-hand drawing is also acceptable.

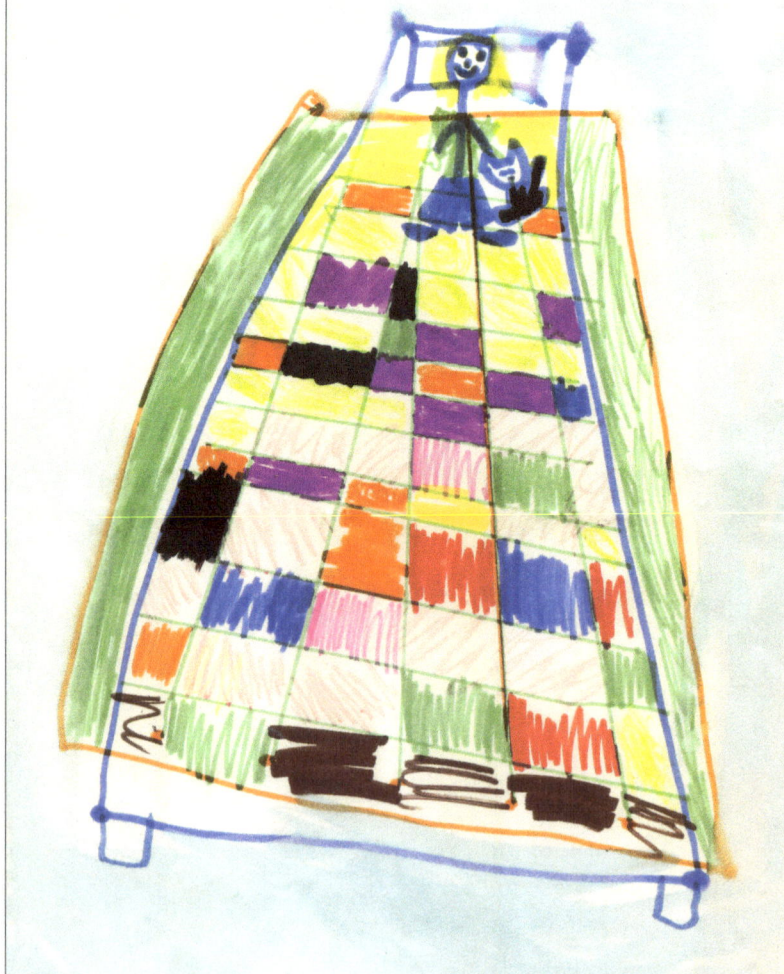

Think: cardboard box. A 1-point perspective shows 1 side of a box, the front. If you see one side, there is one vanishing point on the horizon line. Place the box in front of the horizon line so the line is running through the box. This is easier to draw at first than having the horizon line running above or below the box.

The first rule to remember is: All vertical lines are parallel to each other. If the left side of the box is seen, the vanishing point is to the left of the box. Then draw lines from the left vertical end points to the left vanishing point. We do the same to the right, drawing lines from the right vertical end points to the right vanishing point.

Marking these end points is critical. It is the hardest step in the process. Even marking them in color works at first. These are the end points from which we attach our lines out to the disappearing point. These lines will be diagonal. Now, we connect our diagonal lines to each other with a vertical line. Remember, all vertical lines will be parallel to each other.

Level 3

Visual Space
2-Point Perspective

2-point perspective is the most commonly used in art and drafting. Using the "cardboard box" shape again as your subject, draw a vertical line that is cross-sectioned in the center by a horizontal line. There are two "disappearing points" on the horizon line where the parallel lines appear to meet. By changing the points on the horizontal line, you are able to increase or decrease the size of the object you are drawing. By changing the points on the vertical line, you are able to increase or decrease the nearness of the object to the viewer's eye. Remember: All vertical lines are parallel to each other.

In this example, we see that the vertical lines are symmetrical and evenly spaced. They are also the same in height as they are in depth to the horizon line. This makes for an easy example of how to use 2-point perspective. Notice the lines of the windows and door: the vertical lines are parallel to each other and the horizontal lines all point to the "disappearing points" on the horizon.

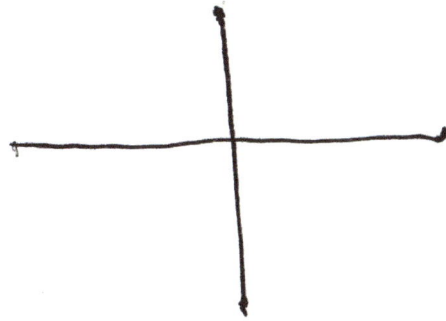

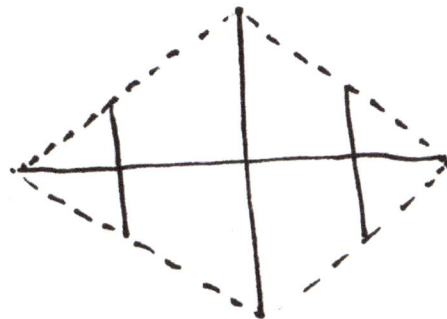

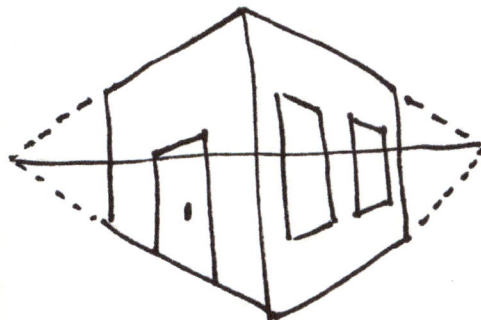

Level 3

Visual Space **3-Point Perspective**

Distance: 3-Point Perspective is a fairly accurate representation of what we see with our eyes.

After mastering 1- and 2-point perspective, we can decide when we feel our students are ready to tackle 3-point perspective. 3-point perspective looks down on the scene from a vantage point above. 3-point perspective sees three sides of a structure, two sides and the roof, so it uses three vanishing points.

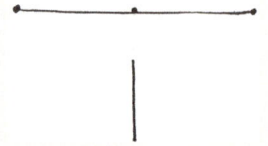

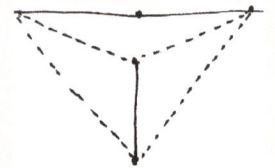

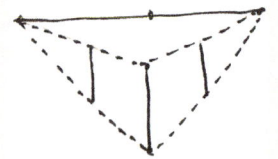

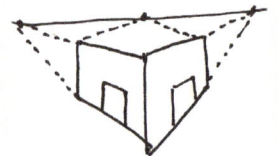

Visual Space **Linear Perspective**

Linear perspective in drawing or painting is a set of rules used to draw 3-dimensional objects on a flat (2-dimensional) surface. The subject can be quite elaborate but luckily you don't need to become an expert to be able to draw well. There are 2 basic rules of linear perspective that you need to remember:

Objects that are closer appear bigger and parallel lines intersect at the horizon.

Level 3

Visual Space **Frame Within a Frame**

This is framing the subject of a picture inside a frame that already exists inside of the picture. It's like looking through an arbor to the garden beyond, or viewing Yosemite through its tunnel approach. It carries the eye straight through from the foreground to the background. We seem to be stepping back a few paces before walking through to the view beyond. It is a technique that is always dramatic. It's often used in filming to suggest connections.

The frame within-a-frame technique usually uses the reverse distance coloring. The grayed, darker, blurred images are in the closer "frame" area and the image inside of the frame is brighter and in focus. The inside image then contains all of the usual Visual Literacy rules of a separate picture.

Level 3

Visual Space **Contrasts**

Level 3

Visual Space Contrasts

"Ironically, it's the departure from symmetry and symmetry breaking that makes life possible." -- John D. Barrows

Looking at turbulence, such as swirls of water, billows of clouds, and clumps of lichen thrusts us into a right brain mode. We can see the two systems, linear and non-linear, that operate simultaneously in our world by observing houses built on physics and clouds above them swirling within geometry.

Mixed up, disorganized patterns can be observed in swirling floating oil, eddies, lava flows, and weather. It is what we "see" in scribble pictures.

For my school group of six children, from kindergarten to grade five, I brought in a pile of picture segments torn from magazines, because of their brilliant color, paper weight, and great pattern images.

Their job was to paste pictures together according to the color contrast of their edge line colors: dark color to light color, and light edge line to dark. They dove into it.

When they were finished pasting, we looked at the pictures. Then we took yogurt cartons half full with white, brown, and turquoise paint – and alternately dribbled, spattered, and poured. It was great fun.

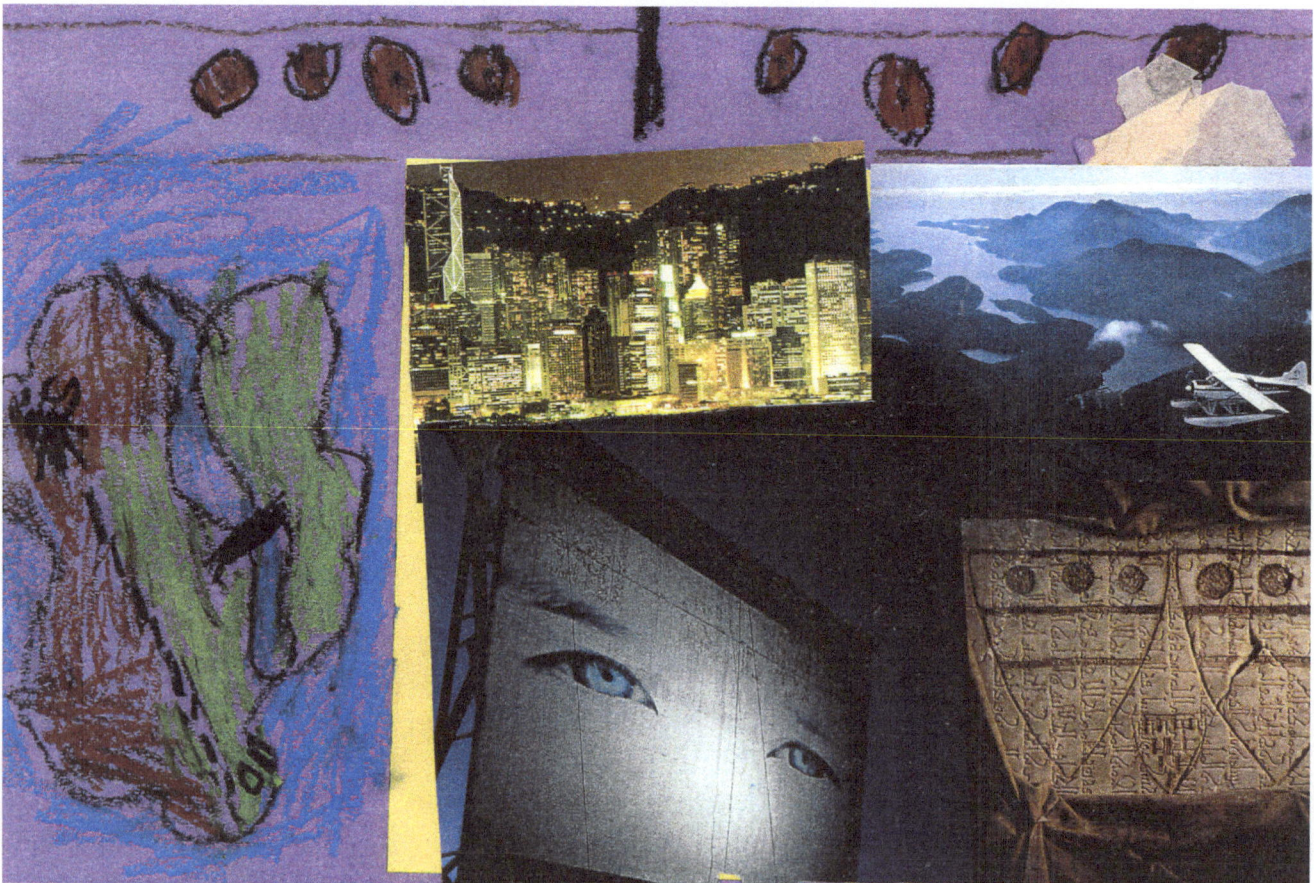

Visual Space Random Placement

Van Gogh's "Starry, Starry Night" as a study in technique and random placement

Stars were cut out, thrown at random, connected geometrically from center point to center point, measured, and then imagined and named as a constellation.

Level 3

Visual Space Fractured Frames

Fractured frames have no easily accessible focal points. They start playing with our brains. We keep looking for connections. Their messages become subliminal. We find that we can accept more information in one flat plane image than we thought.

Artist's have always been the avant garde of possibility thinking. They play endlessly with "I wonder if I …

… took a photo, made several copies, cut them up, fractured the image, and repositioned them"…

… cut them into straight strips but alternated the edges"…

… cut them into uneven shaped strips"…

… alternated the strips with strips from another, but related, picture"…

… cut the strips into wavy, uneven lines"…

… laid the strips in layers horizontally"…

5th Grade. What began as a copy of a Matisse portrait ended with a tiger head.

Level 3

Visual Space Documentation/Making Connections

When the artwork is complete, having your students write on the back can reinforce the links between art and math, science, social studies and language arts. Students will begin to see the connection between what they create and the world around them - the "Bigger Picture".

This is my dog I made and I
love it. It is formal and all vertical.
We were study symmetry.

$$\boxed{X} + \boxed{Y} = \boxed{Y} + \boxed{X}$$
$$a \quad \boxed{3} + \boxed{9} = \boxed{9} + \boxed{3} \quad b$$
$$\boxed{Y} - \boxed{X} = \boxed{X} - \boxed{Y}$$
$$6 \quad \boxed{9} - \boxed{3} = \boxed{3} - \boxed{9} - 6$$

$$\boxed{} + \boxed{} \text{ etc.}$$
Symmetry in math.

Still Life
re-drawn from
memory.

5th gr.

Visual Space **Abstract Art**

What is going on here anyway?

There are no figures or buildings. No shadows, no background, no center of interest. Children actually love doing this kind of art.

While early artists and artisans employed abstract patterns, such as leaves and flowers, as an overall art form, the term "abstract" didn't appear until the 1920's.

More Than Just Pretty Pictures…

Children's art is continually at play and the fun part is that we get a chance to play along with it.

We cannot create without underlying art concepts. But art teachers are few and far between, which is why this book was written. It is here to help you discover the joy in children's art and to embrace the multitude of methods and art forms that can be created.

"It is art that makes life, makes interest, makes importance and, I know of no substitute whatever for the force and beauty of its process."

MAX EASTMAN

All we need do is play at the process. And what a magnificent process it is!

www.ingramcontent.com/pod-product-compliance
Lightning Source LLC
Chambersburg PA
CBHW061055090426
42742CB00002B/46